The Children of MOROCCO

THE WORLD'S CHILDREN

The Children of MOROCCO

JULES HERMES

Carolrhoda Books, Inc./Minneapolis

For Aric, Cristin, Joseph, Meghan, Kerry, Andrew, Holly, David, Jeanne, and Justin

Carolrhoda Books Inc. c/o The Lerner Group
241 First Avenue North, Minneapolis, MN 55401

LIBRARY OF CONGRESS CATALOGING-IN-PUBLICATION DATA

Hermes, Jules, 1962-
  The children of morocco / by Jules Hermes
    p. cm. — (The World's children)
  Includes index.
  ISBN 0-87614-857-7
  1. Morocco—Social life and customs—Juvenile literature.
  2. Children—Morocco—Juvenile literature. I. Title.
  II. Series: World's children (Minneapolis, Minn.)
DT312.H47 1994
964—dc20   94-12709
                                                   CIP
                                                    AC

Manufactured in the United States of America

1 2 3 4 5 6 – I/JR – 00 99 98 97 96 95

The Children of MOROCCO

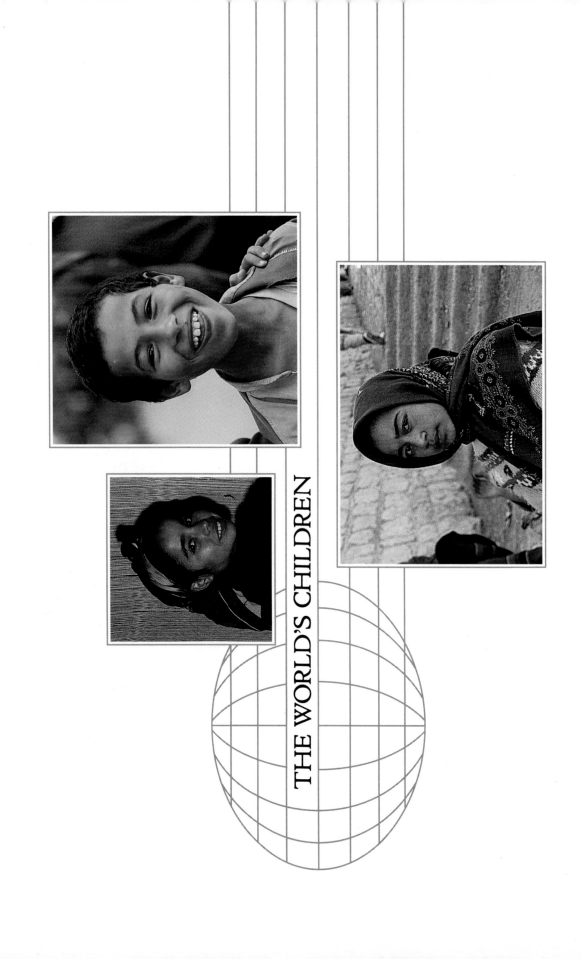

THE WORLD'S CHILDREN

Author's Note:

When I first heard of the country of Morocco, images of mysteriously robed men and veiled women filled my mind. I knew little of this corner of northern Africa and less of the people who live there. When I visited Morocco, I saw an exotic mix of African, Arab, Berber, and European influences. Although the population of 27 million people are divided by race, custom, and origin, they are united by their faith in Islam. Nearly 100 percent Islamic, their religion gives the Moroccan people stability and security in a world in constant conflict. Islam provides them with a sense of belonging, not only to a common faith, but to a common family, and they guard this bond like a precious jewel. When I tried to take a closer look into the lives of the children of Morocco, I found the children were shy. At first I took this shyness as a sign that they did not welcome me. But I soon understood that their reserve is a part of their culture and who they are, and I learned to adapt to their ways of life. To some extent Morocco still is, and always will be, a mystery to me. By tightly guarding their society, Moroccans are preserving their culture for future generations—a culture as fascinating and puzzling as the tangled alleyways of their ancient cities.

Deep in the south of the kingdom of Morocco lies the great Sahara desert, its golden sands stretching thousands of miles across the Maghreb. The Maghreb, an Arabic term meaning west where the sun sets, is a region in North Africa that includes Morocco and its neighbors—Algeria and Tunisia.

The history of this part of the world dates back thousands of years. As early as 2000 B.C., the Berbers have lived in North Africa, fiercely defending themselves from invading Arab and European nations. Many of the people who live in Morocco today are Berbers.

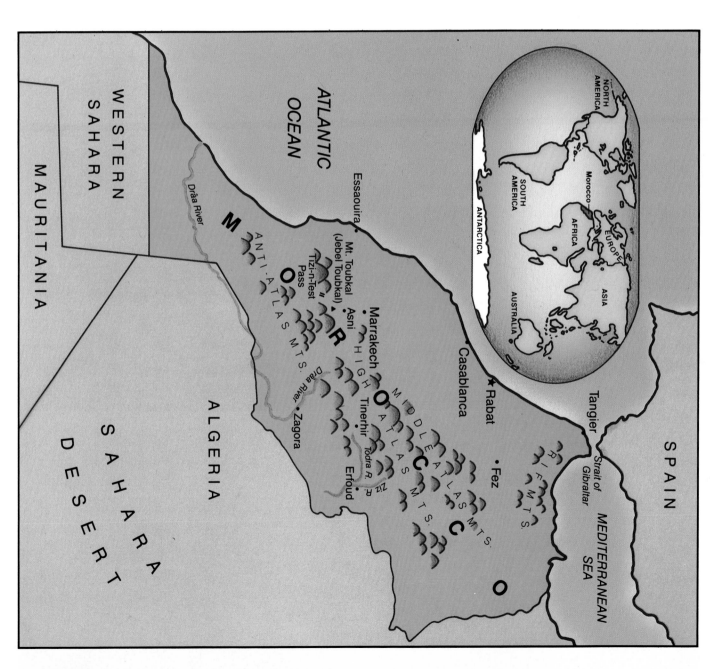

A Berber tent on the edge of the great Sahara desert in southern Morocco

Fatima's father prepares mint tea, the traditional Moroccan drink. Moroccans say that no two people prepare mint tea exactly the same. Depending on the amount of sugar, mint, and the height of the stream of steaming tea as it is poured, each glass has a unique flavor.

Fatima's mother herds their camels in the Sahara.

8

Four-year-old Fatima is a Berber girl whose family are nomads. Fatima and her family live in a Berber tent, just as her ancestors did centuries ago. Fatima's mother and father raise and sell camels, while Fatima and her brother sell handmade Berber dolls to tourists who have come to the desert. Fatima's family has few belongings—their camels are the family's wealth. One camel can fetch enough money for them to live on for several months. Fatima's family chooses to be on their own, away from other people much of the time. Their camels, however, will never go anywhere without at least one other camel. If Fatima's father needs to drive one camel into town, he must find another camel to go along to keep the camel company.

Fatima and her family move several times each year with the change of seasons. When the windy season arrives, the family must move or face the danger of being buried in a sandstorm. During the intensely hot summer months, they move to the cool Atlas Mountains.

Many Berbers live together in casbahs, mud-brick fortresses with high protective walls. Fourteen-year-old Samir lives in a casbah in the town of Erfoud. Every morning Samir's mother sweeps the smooth dirt floors of their house, which are tightly packed by the trampling of many feet over the years. Samir follows the narrow passageways between the houses to buy bread at the casbah's bakery. After breakfast, Samir works at the casbah's olive oil press. The olives are crushed beneath a stone, which is turned by the donkey that Samir leads in a circle around the press. The olive oil is drained, bottled, and sold to other countries. Selling olive oil is one of the ways that the casbah supports itself. The people grow their own food and look after each other. They rarely leave the casbah, except to buy extra supplies or to sell their goods at a larger market.

Casbahs dot the landscape of the Drâa and Ziz valleys of southern Morocco.

Olives are pressed to make olive oil
sold throughout Morocco and abroad.

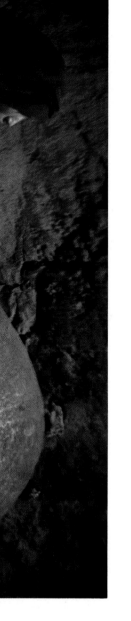

A Berber woman of the Erfoud casbah
makes fresh bread in the bakery.

Batoul's father loads his newly purchased lamb on his moped.

Batoul's mother joins other women of their village at the Zagora market where they sell baskets and silver jewelry.

In the deep south, Moroccans travel from their villages to the weekly market. On market day, Batoul and her mother leave their casbah in Amezrou to walk the four miles to the market in Zagora. Each week they bring baskets, silver, and fruit to sell. With the money they make, Batoul's father buys food for the family. This week he buys a lamb and loads it onto his moped. Most Berbers use only donkeys or camels for transportation. Batoul considers her family very lucky to have a moped to carry goods to and from their casbah.

Batoul

13

Most Moroccans consider themselves either Berbers or Arabs. About 1,200 years ago, Arab armies swept across North Africa, making it part of the Arab empire and spreading their religion, called Islam. Arabs make up the majority of Morocco's population of about 27 million people. Now nearly 99 percent of all Moroccans—Arabs and Berbers alike—are Muslims, followers of the Islamic religion.

Twelve-year-old Driss works in Marrakech as a gravestone carver. He carves religious verses from the Koran, the holy book of the Muslims, into the marble gravestones. When Muslims die, they are buried with their feet facing Mecca. Mecca, located in Saudi Arabia, is the Muslims' holiest city. Driss has never been there, but he will make a pilgrimage (called the *hajj*) to Mecca once in his lifetime, as do most Muslims.

Five times each day, Driss listens for the muezzin's call to prayer. A muezzin calls out from each neighborhood mosque, which is the central place of Muslim worship. When Driss hears the call to prayer, he faces Mecca and recites this prayer in Arabic: "There is no God but Allah, and Muhammad is his prophet." Driss, like most Muslims, believes that his God is the same God of the Christians and Jews, and that Muhammad is a prophet of God.

Driss

From the mosque, the muezzin calls the people to prayer at dawn, noon, mid-afternoon, early evening, and nightfall.

14

Muslims take a break from their chores when called to prayer from the fields.

Djemaa el Fna

16

The heart of Marrakech is the
old city, and the heart of the old
city is Djemaa el Fna, a huge
square filled with vendors, per-
formers, snake charmers, and
dancers. Meena and her brother,
Maarou-Fa, spend most evenings
at the square with their parents.
They come to the square most-
ly to listen to the storytellers. For
centuries the storytellers have
gathered large crowds in the
Djemaa el Fna. They begin a
story and continue the same
story for months. People return
night after night to hear the next
part of the story. After the sun
goes down, Meena and Maarou-
Fa like to eat kabobs from one
of the dozens of vendors who
have set up their large tents for
the evening.

Meena and Maarou-Fa

Meena and Maarou-Fa's father sells medicines and their mother sells handwoven baskets in the Djemaa el Fna. Their friend, Hareesh, performs acrobatics in the square. Over 100 people at a time gather to watch Hareesh perform throughout the evening. If they like his performance, they toss money into his hat. On a good day, he can make 50 dirhams, about $6.00. The dirham is the unit of currency in Morocco, and eight dirhams equals about one U.S. dollar.

Hareesh likes to feel the excitement in the air at the Djemaa el Fna square. Although it is mandatory for all children to attend school until the age of 13, Hareesh, 12, does not go to school because he feels he can make a better living as a performer. Hareesh's parents consider him an adult and old enough to make his own choices about his life.

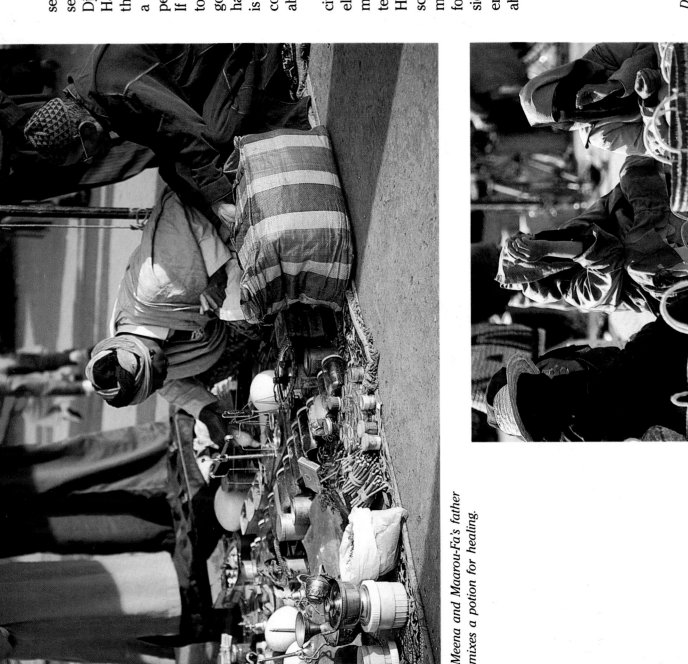

Meena and Maarou-Fa's father mixes a potion for healing.

Dressed in traditional Moroccan clothing, Meena and Maarou-Fa's mother sells handwoven baskets.

Hareesh performs in the Djemaa el Fna.

Drissia works at the carpet factory. Moroccan carpets, woven only by women, are sold in almost every Moroccan town or city.

Thirteen-year-old Drissia also lives in Marrakech. For hundreds of years, the women in Drissia's family have learned to weave carpets from their mothers. In Moroccan homes, carpets are used not only as floor coverings, but also as chairs and beds.

Drissia goes to school in the afternoons and, in the mornings, she weaves carpets at a factory. Women weave the carpets by hand creating intricate designs that often take several months to complete. Drissia and her friends use looms and work in small, poorly lit rooms at a carpet factory. Although the factory owners sell the carpets for up to $5,000, they pay the weavers only about $1.00 per day. Despite the tedious work and low pay, Drissia takes pride in the quality of the carpets she produces.

The Ville Nouvelle, or New Marrakech, has modern hotels, restaurants, and shops.

The village of Moulay Brahim

Just as Drissia has learned to weave, many girls learn the art of tattooing. Isha lives in the High Atlas Mountains above Marrakech in a village called Moulay Brahim. Isha tattoos her mother's hands with henna, a dye that colors the skin a deep reddish orange. Women of Moulay Brahim are famous for their ability to tattoo with henna. Some women come from 50 miles away to have their hands and feet tattooed in Moulay Brahim. Isha learned the art from her mother. First she mixes the henna with water to create a muddy substance. Then she squeezes the henna through a tube and onto the hands, creating lacy geometric patterns. Each of the intricate designs has a symbolic meaning. Then Isha wraps her mother's hands in soft cotton or gauze. It takes several hours for the henna to dry, but the beautiful tattoos will last about three weeks.

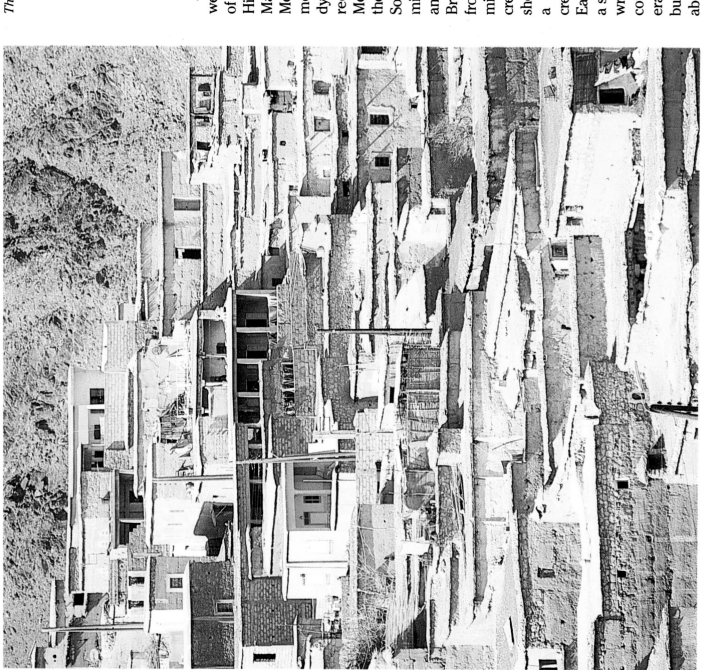

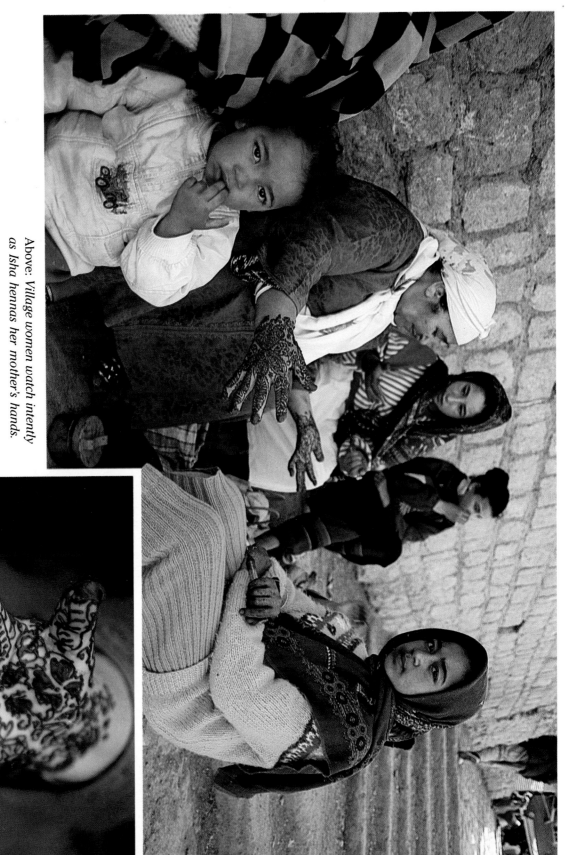

Above: Village women watch intently as Isha hennas her mother's hands.

Right: After this mud-colored henna dries, Isha's mother will wash her hands to reveal the red-orange designs left behind.

Muhammad lives just three miles away from Isha in the village of Asni. He and his grandfather come to the Asni market for supplies and a haircut. Muhammad often has trouble sitting still while the barber uses a blade to cut his hair. He would rather watch the activity in the market. Unlike most other markets in Morocco, however, only men are allowed to attend the Asni market. Muhammad's mother and sisters stay at home doing chores, as do the other women in Asni and the surrounding villages. Men bring fresh produce, spices, and animals to the market hoping to sell everything they have brought. After they make their purchases, Muhammad and his grandfather treat themselves to lunch and listen to the musicians who play throughout the market.

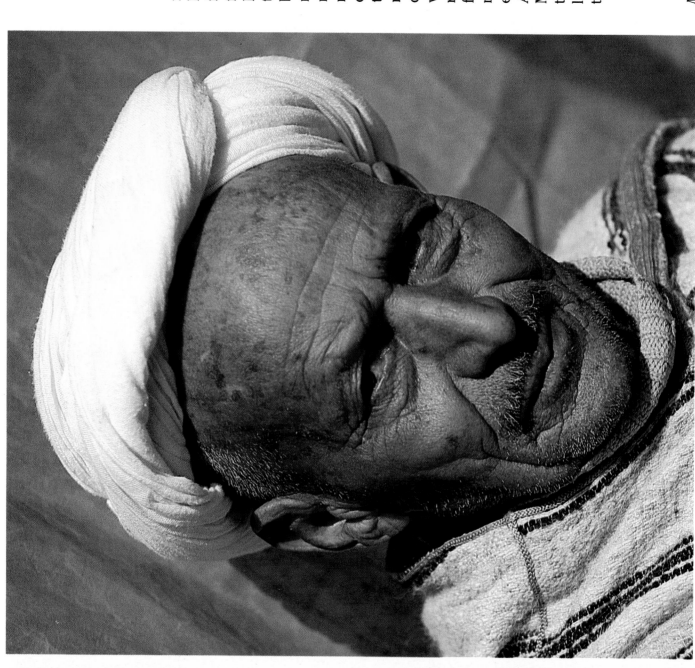

Muhammad's grandfather

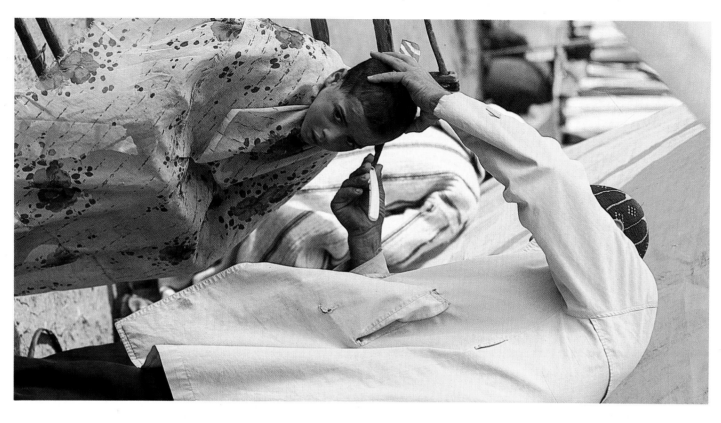

The Asni market is one of the few markets in Morocco that only men can attend.

Muhammad squirms during his haircut.

A village with a clear view of Mount Toubkal

Karija comes from a smaller village near Asni. From her home, Karija has a clear view of Morocco's highest mountain, Mount Toubkal. Karija's father is a blacksmith in the Asni marketplace (also called a souk) where he shoes donkeys and mules. In the fall, Karija's father is very busy preparing the pack animals before the harsh winter months arrive. When heavy snowfall blocks the nearby Tizin-Test pass, only donkeys and mules can make the journey along the narrow ledges of the mountain roads. In the spring and summer, however, many foreigners pass through Asni on their way to climb Mount Toubkal, which rises over 13,000 feet.

Karija

Karija's father shoes donkeys in the souk.

Left: *Hazeem herds his sheep through the Todra Gorge.*
Opposite page: *A village in the Todra Gorge*

The Tizi-n-Test pass cuts through the lushly green heart of the High Atlas Mountains. The rocky and barren land to the south has a beauty all its own. Hazeem comes from one of southern Morocco's most spectacular sights—the Todra Gorge. Mud and clay villages sit at the bottom of the gorge surrounded by sheer rock walls that rise nearly one thousand feet straight up. Several times during the year, Hazeem and his father must herd their flock of sheep through the gorge to the nearest town of Tinerhir where the flock will be sold. Along the isolated road to Tinerhir, Hazeem and his father pass only one village where they can get water for the ten-mile walk.

The deep gorges of the south create rivers and streams that wind their way to the Atlantic ocean. Harija and Sayeeda live in Essaouira, a port town on the coast of the Atlantic that was built by the Portuguese in the 16th century. Harija and Sayeeda spend their days down by the pier, where their father works on a large fishing boat. The life of a fisherman can be dangerous and Harija and

Looking out to the ocean from Essaouira. Inset: *Harija and Sayeeda*

Sayeeda worry about their father's safety, especially when the ocean shows its power. They believe their father will remain safe, *inshallah. Inshallah* means "God (Allah) willing", and Muslims exchange these words many times each day. For Sayeeda and Harija, their faith in Allah and their commitment to their family affect every part of their lives.

Harija and Sayeeda's father returns to the port after a week of fishing.

Schoolchildren from Marrakech learn about Essaouira's history as they walk along the ramparts and down by the pier.

The influence of the Muslim faith can be seen throughout Morocco. Even in Casablanca, Morocco's largest city, Muslim holidays are strictly observed. During Ramadan, the ninth month of the Muslim calendar, the amusement park in the heart of Casablanca is empty. During Ramadan all Muslims must not eat or drink anything from dawn to dusk. Ramadan is observed by Muslims to commemorate the period in which the Koran, or sacred teachings, were revealed to the prophet Muhammad by God.

Yassin and Yunis

During the rest of the year, many children who live in Casablanca play in the amusement park, especially those who live in the nearby affluent neighborhoods. Yassin and Yunis often stop in the park on their way home from school. Sometimes they go on the rides, but most of the time they like to just sit and watch the people go by. With a population of two and a half million people and visitors from around the world, Casablanca is a great place for people watching.

Above, left: People stroll past the outdoor cafes and shops that line the pedestrian district of Casablanca.

Above, right: Because many people of Casablanca speak French and conduct business in French, the road signs are in French, as well as Arabic.

Right: A young girl and her mother search for the right souvenir as they leave the children's amusement park.

The official language of Morocco is Arabic, but most Moroccans also speak French because France ruled Morocco from 1912 to 1956. During that time, many Moroccan cities were rebuilt using French cities as their model with tree-lined avenues, beautiful parks, and outdoor cafes. Morocco's capital, Rabat, is one of the four imperial cities of the kingdom of Morocco. King Hassan II, the spiritual leader and political ruler of Morocco, lives in a grand palace. Many people who live in Rabat work for the government and live in comfortable apartments and homes.

As in most of the large cities in the world, wealth and poverty exist side by side in Rabat. Even though some families have only enough money for food and other essentials, they still give money to others less fortunate than themselves. This is called giving alms, and it is an important part of the Muslim religion.

Homelessness is a problem in Rabat, just as it is in many large cities in other parts of the world.

At the same time that France ruled Morocco, the northern port city of Tangier became an international zone. As a result, Tangier was considered the gateway for thousands of French and other European people to settle in Tangier and other parts of Morocco. Many Moroccans learned to speak French and continue to do so today.

Aziza lives in Tangier and speaks fluent French as well as Arabic and some Spanish. On warm spring evenings, Aziza and her sisters walk to the port and watch the ships bringing passengers to Morocco from Spain. Aziza likes to meet the tourists who come to Tangier, often for just a half-day visit. From high atop the *jebels*, or hills, above Tangier, Aziza can see Spain, only about eight miles away on the other side of the Strait of Gibraltar.

Tangier is the closest port between the African continent and Europe and receives thousands of visitors each day.

A view of Tangier from the hillsides

Ahmed and his grandmother

While Tangier was an international zone, Spain ruled some areas outside the city. Where Ahmed lives in the Rif Mountains outside Tangier, many people still speak Spanish. Ahmed's grandmother is Andalusian, a person from a southern region of Spain. She wears traditional Andalusian clothing every day, but Ahmed prefers western-style clothing. Ahmed and his grandmother operate what they call a roadside cafe. Each day they pick fresh cactus fruit and prepare it with a grain cereal and goat's milk to serve for breakfast at their cafe. A full breakfast or lunch costs about eight dirhams, or $1.00.

Moroccan tourists stop for lunch at Ahmed's roadside cafe.

The mouth of Hercules' Cave, located outside of Tangier, resembles the shape of the African continent.

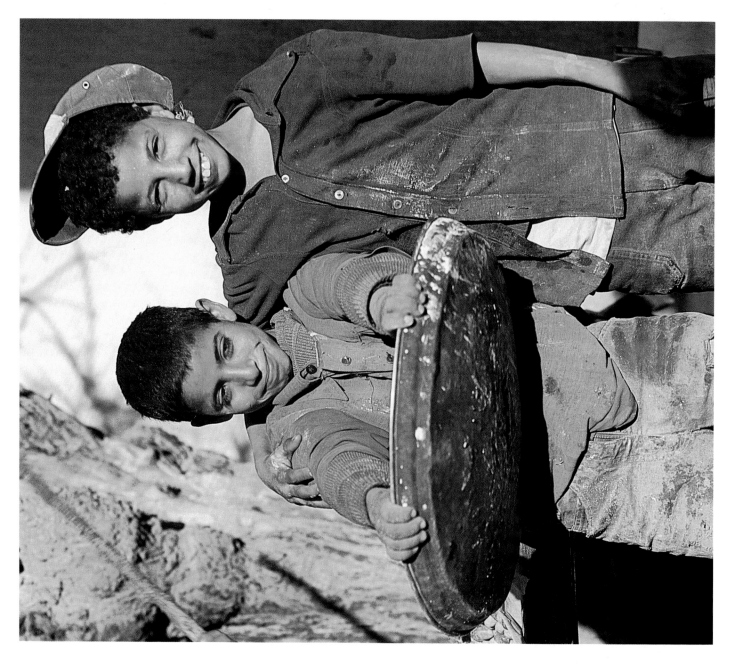

Hakim and his brother

Hakim lives in Fez, one of the oldest cities in Morocco. Fez, like many other large Moroccan cities, has two parts to it: the medina, or old city, and the ville nouvelle, or new city. The oldest part of the city of Fez was founded in A.D. 790 and is called the medina of Fez el-Bali. Hakim and his brother sell roasted nuts and fruits in the medina, as boys have done for centuries. Little in the medina has changed since Hakim's ancesters lived in Fez—craft shops line the marketplace and donkeys lumber past, their hooves clattering on the cobblestone streets. Hakim and other boys learn their fathers' trades not only to support themselves in the future, but also to contribute money for their families to live on.

Said's father teaches him to carve wood.

Hakim's friend Said works as a carver in the woodcarvers' souk. Said carves elaborate tables and shelves out of cedar trees in a traditional Moroccan style. To find the woodcarvers' souk, a tourist must follow the pungent aroma of cedar, since there are no signs or directions to point the way. Around every corner of the winding cobblestone paths are new sights and smells leading to the leather, silver, and pottery souks, and the main mosque in the center.

Only a bit of dim sunlight seeps into the cramped space between the buildings and the walls of the medina. Women sit in the cool, dark souk selling bread.

Fez has the largest leather tannery in Morocco. Here animal skins are dyed and then sent to craftsmen who will make handbags, clothing, and other items out of the skins. Fifteen-year-old Abdul Fakir makes his living working in the tannery. Each day, instead of going to school, he works nearly 10 hours, knee-deep in a clay hole filled with leather dye. He stomps on the skins, soaking them with the dye. When the dye has completely drenched the skins, Abdul stretches the skins and lays them to dry in the hot sun on the rooftop of the tannery. The long days and sometimes unbearable stench make Abdul's job difficult. He can't quit his job, though, because he needs the money to survive on his own. And, being friends with the other boys who work at the tannery makes each day go by more quickly.

Fez tannery

Abdul takes a break from stomping skins in a hole full of dye. His legs stay stained from the dye.

Young boys lay dyed skins on the tannery rooftop to dry in the hot sun.

Life in Fez is typical of most Moroccan cities. While many Fassi children go to school and live in comfortable homes, many more children are already working. Even very young children in poor and working class families learn the trades of their mothers and fathers to secure not only their own futures, but their families' futures as well. Many work long hours in harsh conditions, but they do not consider this a hardship. They feel that working is their duty to their families and Allah.

Like Abdul Fakir, Said, and Hakim, many children of Morocco must take on a great deal of responsibility in their everyday lives. They have little time to think of things they want or what they would like out of life. Instead they think about what they can give to the lives of the people around them and to Allah. Five times each day when they hear the muezzin's prayer call from high atop the minaret of the mosque, they kneel in prayer and place their faith for the future in the hands of Allah.

Fez

The constant motion of people mixes with the multitude of sounds and scents in the medina of Old Fez.

45

More Facts about Morocco

How many people live in Morocco?
Morocco is home to about 27 million people.

How big is Morocco?
Morocco covers 174,000 square miles, an area that is slightly larger than the state of California.

Which Moroccan city has the largest population?
Casablanca's population of 2.5 million people makes it Morocco's largest city.

What form of government does Morocco have?
Morocco is a constitutional monarchy headed by a king. Morocco's constitution, which was approved by popular vote in 1972, gives the king broad powers. The king appoints a prime minister and other cabinet ministers. The Chamber of Representatives makes Morocco's laws, and two-thirds of the Chamber of Representatives are elected by the people.

What is Morocco's main industry?
Phosphate rock, a key ingredient in fertilizers, is Morocco's greatest natural asset. The world purchases over 40 percent of its phosphate from Morocco. The largest phosphate deposits in the world are mined in Morocco.

Index